All the best.

# MAKE YOURSELF
# AGELESS

*366 Ways To keep Growing Young*

## BRUCE S. GARRABRANDT

*Other books by Bruce Garrabrandt*

**The Power of Having Desire**

**Cattle Drive** (And 153 Other Random Acts of Artistic Nonsense)

**My Name Is On The Deed...But The Cats Own The House**

*For Jean Marie Woolley, a gentle teacher who demonstrates this life truth daily: Our biggest moments always involve the smallest acts of love.*

## ACKNOWLEDGEMENTS

*Special thanks to Jeffrey White, of White Custom Media, for fashioning my words and chosen illustrations into a visual work of art.*

*I am also grateful to Gayle L. Garrabrandt for her helpful editorial suggestions in preparation of the final manuscript.*

*For the use of the line art illustrations found throughout these pages, I should also like to thank Harold H. Hart, editor of The Picture Reference File, Vols. I & II, (Hart Publishing Co., Inc., NYC 1976.)*

# INTRODUCTION

This is a book about artful living for people in mid-life and beyond. (With 138,000,000 Americans over the age of forty, I'm hoping this little volume stays in print for a long time.)

"I can't even draw a straight line" is a comment I hear often as a professional artist. Well, I suggest you embrace this as your personal life prescription, and keep away from straight lines. They represent habitual, routine paths. Fill your days with curves, spikes, and swirls. Practice fanciful loops in all sorts of shapes and sizes.

Recently, a woman came into my booth at an arts festival and sighed, "In my next life I want to come back with talent."

"Why wait?" I asked. "Go for it now."

I'm an artist who began with no talent for drawing, and an author who had no innate ability to write. A passion to learn these skills, and the willingness to work through frustrations and setbacks, took me to where I wanted to be. Please don't think this is boasting. I'm a man of average intelligence. (My friends would argue I'm boasting when I say *that*.)

Trust me—if someone as flawed and absent-minded as I am can transform desires into talents, *anyone* can. We tend to look at people who excel—in any field— and think, "What wonderful talents they were born with." Sometimes this is true. Most times it's not.

Talented people arrived here gifted with what everyone possesses at birth—unique passions, and the potential to develop them. When we see accomplished people, we're usually observing results, not inborn talents. We're looking at individuals who were committed to doing things, clumsily at first, but persevered until they could do them well.

When I ask classical musicians, "Were you born with a talent for the instrument?," most answer without hesitation, "No—I was born with a *love* for the instrument…and I played it horribly. But I kept playing it, hours every day, for twenty years."

Mozart could compose and play minuets at age three. He was born with innate talent. If all other classical musicians compared themselves to Mozart, we'd only have Mozart. Inborn talent is wonderful, but it's not a prerequisite for success. What is required is passionate commitment to a dream.

When my first book, ***The Power of Having Desire***, was published in 2004, reporters interviewing me listened politely while I explained how passion—not talent—is the key to success, citing my own artistic journey as an example. Only after 10,000 hours of practice at the easel, I told them, did I gain an ability to draw well.

More than one reporter shook his head at this, saying, "I could spend 10,000 hours drawing, but I'd be no good at it. My talent is for writing."

"Really?" I asked. "Tell me—were you born with that talent?" No writer (not even Shakespeare) was born with an ability to write. None of us even knows about language at birth. What writers exhibit early is a love for words and the desire to put them together in meaningful ways. No child does this well at age two; but, if words are your passion and you long to write well—then, by the time you've reached thirty-two, you're probably earning your living as a writer.

What talent or ability do you long to possess? Be willing to do a thing badly...*and keep doing it.* Commitment to a cherished desire, with disciplined perseverance, is essential to success in any endeavor. Stay on course and new talents will emerge. Look silly for now. It's one of the best ways to keep growing young.

*Be willing to do a thing badly...and keep doing it.*

Comedian Steve Allen began his career in radio during the 1940's. He was one of the first entertainers to take a microphone into the studio audience and interview visitors to his program. His quick wit and command of the English language enabled him to engage in playful ad-libbing. One of his favorite gags involved asking an older audience member, "What do you do for a living?" If the person answered, "I'm retired," Steve would quip, "I wondered why you were here in your pajamas."

Keep in mind that one definition of "retire" is to go to sleep. I don't know who first chose this awful word to describe that time when people leave their careers. It connotes an ending rather than a beginning. With the richest language in the world, surely we can find better words to describe a stage of life that holds an abundance of possibilities. I humbly offer some suggestions throughout this book, but I urge you to find your own substitutes for the sleepy "retire."

Character actress Ruth Gordon, best remembered for her roles in *Rosemary's Baby* and *Harold and Maude*, was a frequent guest on late-night TV talk shows in the 1970's. One evening, while discussing her career and current projects, the animated, enthusiastic Miss Gordon turned to host Dick Cavett and proclaimed, "I made up my mind years ago—I will grow older, but I will *never* grow old." She stayed true to this pledge.

Youthful spirit and a love of life accompanied her to the finish line.

When I.A. Stone ended his long career in journalism, friends asked about his plans for the future. His reply: "I want to die young as late as possible." Make this your goal, too.

Welcome to half-time. Now is your best opportunity, while the band is playing, to compose and perform your own music. What follows are 366 ways to help you play the second half as your soulful half.

## 1.

Each of us is born a unique individual. Look within any family: Siblings living under the same roof, nurtured by the same parents, nevertheless exhibit distinct personalities. More than mere birth order is at work here. Everyone is fashioned for specific purposes.

What is your calling? You are alive for a reason, entrusted with *potential* talents and abilities at every age. Identifying and acting on these is your choice. It can only happen if you commit to making it happen.

Malcolm Forbes said, "Success follows doing what you want to do. There is no other way to be successful." Identify personal passions that bring forth attributes and the temperament that are uniquely yours. Discover callings that resonate for you in a deeply meaningful way. You will never need to reinvent yourself: You will be living your *authentic* self.

## 2.

Drop "retire" and substitute "renew."

## 3.

A calling revealed—and reveled in—employs heart and mind in a higher purpose. Get engaged in what absorbs and excites you. You'll bring joy and fulfillment to your daily journey, while serving as a loving catalyst for others, encouraging them, by example, to see life in a broader, richer context.

**4.**

*I was always at the foot of the class.*
--Thomas Edison

Curiosity and commitment to creativity, through *self* education, is more important than formal education. The soul knows what excites it and avoids subjects irrelevant to its mission. Identify what captivates you and surrender to it with the self-motivation that accompanies passion—and watch your creativity soar. This is your calling.

## 5.

Exceptional people point the way for the rest of us, because they reveal, sometimes at an early age, the truth that the embryo of excellence is harbored within each of us. Potential capabilities lie slumbering—waiting for us to awaken and nurture them.

Inherent in the artistic expression of others is this unspoken message, aimed directly at you: Commit to *your* creativity and make artful contributions to life.

## 6.

Make creative geniuses your unwitting spiritual guides. Listen to 16-year-old Judy Garland sing *Over the Rainbow*. Watch Gene Kelly dance with his umbrella in *Singin' in the Rain*. Read the poem that we have labeled *The Gettysburg Address*. (Pay attention to the structure, rhythm and cadence of Lincoln's words. He was truly our poet-president.)

## 7.

Individuality gives each person the opportunity to contribute to life in distinctly personal ways. Commitment to your creative spirit feeds the nonconformist soul. When built upon a spiritual foundation, it shapes character and provides an ongoing awareness that life is your singular calling—no matter what your occupation. See yourself as the miracle of creation you are.

Why are we obsessed with "3?" Genies give us three wishes. Joke construction usually consists of three parts. "Three" appears in stories, songs and movie titles, and in everyday speech far more than does any other number. Here's just a sampling:

*The Three Little Pigs*
*Three Blind Mice*
*Goldilocks and the Three Bears*
*The Three Wise Men*
*The Three Faces of Eve*
*Three Coins in the Fountain*
*Three Little Words*
*The Three Musketeers*
*Three Dog Night*
*Three sheets to the wind*
*"Three strikes and you're out"*
*"The third time's the charm"*
*"I'll give you three guesses…"*
*"I'll count to three…"*
*"The three 'R's'"*

Why do we feel comfortable—so at home—with this number? Could it be part of our internal wiring? Do genetics, environment, and *inspiration* form us?

Pay attention to your soul. It will shape your destiny. Develop mind, body, and *spirit*. Build yourself upon a spiritual foundation, with awareness. You'll transform every action into a teachable moment.

## 9.

Rooting your life in the temporal will bring devastation during periods of unwanted change and upheaval. Choose an inner, spiritual planting. This ensures deeper growth, anchoring you to weather life's turbulent times.

## 10.

Make yourself available to your inner self. Be on-call to it. Listen to your longings—and act on them. Inspiration awaits your action. Take daily steps toward a personal dream.

What you desire, and commit to with faith, you can bring to fruition.

## 11.

Not in the position to take an extended leave from your current job? Create an early morning sabbatical from sleep. Take time at the start of each day to reflect on your life. Examine your personality. What is most important to you? Write a list of your deepest wishes. Create an honest "personality profile" you can match to work that both suits your personality and fulfills your fundamental needs.

People who say, "I'm too old to learn" are announcing to the world that they have been alive too long to be intelligent, independent, reasoning human beings. Huh?

Should you find yourself thinking, "I'm too old to learn something new," stop and take your pulse. If you still have one, you can (and should) be learning something new.

Follow your passions and forget your years.

## 13.

Now is the time to embrace your second childhood—by returning to your first one. Reawaken that sense of wonder, curiosity, and discovery you knew as a child. Creative opportunities surround you. An attitude of optimism opens your eyes to them.

## 14.

Instead of "retirement," how about "redirection?" You're not facing an ending, but rather a transformation. Choose to make this a time of exploration and learning.

## 15.

Life owes you nothing. Keep yourself employed in positive pursuits. You'll provide for your needs and know a fulfillment that life offers in no other way.

## 16.

Imagination does not come with an expiration date. Open yourself to new possibilities today.

## 17.

Always show your age—just choose to make it five.

Failure, disappointment, and unfulfilled dreams constitute the unhappy baggage carried by every thoughtful human being by mid-life. Some have a brown bag amount, some a knapsack's worth, and others lug around suitcases crammed full. No one arrives at this point in life without holding some quantity of sadness and regret.

Baggage can be highly useful when examined to glean insight about yourself. The only healthy way to hold onto your past is by embracing lessons learned from having lived it.

Learn the lessons from your baggage, then release your grip—let go—and travel unfettered for the rest of your journey. Keep in mind this reworked cliché from humorist James Thurber: "It's lighter than you think."

## 19.

People tend to pigeon-hole others. Strive always to be categorized as "creative."

## 20.

"Knock knock."
"Who's there?"
"Senile."
"Senile who?"
"You just said that."

Cultivate a sense of humor. It's a key to remaining playful--and mentally young--at *any* age.

## 21.

Each of us needs to love and be loved. Focus on loving more, and "being loved" will take care of itself.

## 22.

It's okay to visit your past, but don't take up permanent residence there. Past used as schoolroom enables you to move forward with wisdom and humility. Dwelling in yesterdays transforms past into prison, locking out the possibility of personal growth.

Live in this present moment and savor it. The most enriching opportunity you'll ever have is now.

# 23.

Discard "retire" and embrace "reanimate."

## 24.

Growing older affords you the opportunity to commune with your life experience. Now you can put it into better perspective, bringing intensity and meaning to what you were too preoccupied to notice at the time you lived through it.

Your knowledge and past, combined with introspection, enable you to make wiser choices, to seek rewarding ways to utilize your unique strengths in service to others.

Age is no roadblock to productive pursuits. On the contrary, the accumulation of years opens countless new roads of possibility to you. Your life experience is a powerful guidance counselor. Consult with it regularly.

## 25.

In youth you sought answers to the cosmic riddle of life. As an older, reflective adult, find contentment in nestling among the questions. Be grateful you are part of a miracle.

## 26.

Individuality and ego blind us to our interconnectedness as human beings. Think of the people involved in supplying your food, shelter, and clothing. The necessities of life, as well as the comforts and conveniences you enjoy, all depend upon the existence—and success—of others. Independence is an illusion.

Try to live entirely alone for a week—not only keeping away from other human beings, but also avoiding anything produced by them. If the crushing loneliness doesn't kill you, starvation or exposure surely will. Be grateful for the interdependence of strangers.

## 27.

Don't just find hobbies—embrace passions. Focus on pursuits that excite you. Choose paths that challenge your mind to stretch beyond its comfort zone. Trust yourself, as well as your multiple decades of life experience, to keep you growing. Fill your days with discovery.

Creativity ascends a spiritual mountain whose peak is sensed in every step. Ironically, that peak grows higher as you climb; however, when the journey enthralls you, the summit becomes secondary.

## 28.

Be filled with awe. Life at its most fundamental level exhibits a dazzling complexity. Study the intricacies of a single cell. See how it is encrypted with a depth of design and information beyond human comprehension. Stay mindful that a wondrous, creative intelligence infuses everything—including *you*.

## 29.

Nurture a heightened awareness of beauty and meaning in the ordinary. Life's simplest moments can bring a sense of fulfillment you never took time to notice or appreciate in youth.

## 30.

One of the few things I remember from college is this line from 18th Century writer Samuel Johnson:

*There is, in man, a longing for which this world holds no gratification.*

I see this unnamed desire as a spiritual longing to connect with something larger than ourselves. The most effective way to do so—on this side of the soil— is to be kind and compassionate to others. Life is either all about love, or it is about nothing.

Choose love daily.

# 31.

Do not let your muscles atrophy or your mind will surely follow.  Turn back the clock on the way you feel—through exercise.  Much to our annoyance, time pushes us forward, but the commitment to a modest exercise program can restore muscle tone, enhance energy, and increase endurance.  Coordination and balance will improve.

Get into shape—and stay that way.

## 32.

Watching television can be great exercise: Just do it from a treadmill. Get moving! Take a proactive approach to your health. It's the best investment you can make—and government has yet to figure a way to tax the dividends.

## 33.

Place a still-life in front of 100 artists and ask them to paint it. You'll get 100 different interpretations of *the same still life*. Each human being possesses a unique set of life experiences.

Use yours in artful ways to inspire others.

## 34.

Creativity is infectious. Your local library is filled with powerful, potential mentors—successful men and women whose wisdom is available to you at no charge. Immerse yourself in their stories. Connect with their genius. Doing so will transform you by strengthening your own imagination and mental capabilities.

## 35.

Make life and laughter inseparable companions. The relationship will enrich all your days.

## 36.

Keep yourself from ever being "over the hill," by choosing higher hills.

## 37.

Put yourself out to pasture only to get more greens in your diet.

## 38.

With youthful obligations and distractions behind you, now is the time to turn outward, to rise above ego and self-interest—just enough to see the interconnectedness of life.

Make it your full-time job to think and act toward others from this perspective. To feel good inside yourself, focus on things outside yourself.

## 39.

Know that any day in which you awaken, no matter how difficult, is a gift to you.

## 40.

If you're not finding some joy in today, perhaps it's time to change your priorities.

## 41.

Opportunities abound, but only when you abandon your resistance to change.

Life is in continual transition and transformation. It's not enough to accept change. Follow its lead and do the same.

## 42.

The shift in seasons demonstrates that the essence of life is change; however, the fact that life is cyclical doesn't mean you should spend yours going in circles.

## 43.

To hasten your education, first slow your pace. Decreasing your speed provides the ideal environment in which to improve your focus and powers of observation. This is the path to heightened awareness.

*To hasten your education, first slow your pace.*

## 44.

Jettison "retire" and take on "reassess."

## 45.

Retirement is impossible if you make a career of personal development. Keep self-improvement a full-time job.

## 46.

Decades devoted to work and family can cause sensory deprivation in us. The hurried pace of daily life, with its relentless routines and pressing obligations, dulls our senses. We're simply too busy to appreciate the myriad of miracles surrounding us.

Now is the time to increase and refine your sensory awareness. Indulge your five senses. Immerse yourself in the subtleties of sight, sound, taste, touch and smell. Cultivate heightened perception.

Your five senses form the rich palette for creative expression. Use them to transform life experience into artful living. The present moment is your canvas. Capture the now vibrantly.

## 47.

The best instant gratification comes when you're fully in the present with a sense of wonder. Be here now.

## 48.

Live by an alternative definition of "supply and demand:" Opportunities for growth and fulfillment lie everywhere—in abundant supply—if you demand the best from yourself.

## 49.

Author Robert Fulghum doesn't like business cards. He thinks they're too confining. "Making a living and having a life are not the same thing," he says. "A job title doesn't even come close to answering the question, 'What do you do?'"

Fulghum is right. "What do you do?" is an expansive question that should start you thinking less about occupations and more about the meaningful ways you spend time. Strive to fill your days with a rich variety of activities, too numerous to list on any business card.

## 50.

You are both teacher and student to everyone you meet. Keep open to this interactive exchange of perceptions and experiences.

## 51.

Find new ways to be useful. Volunteer for organizations or charities whose goals you champion.

## 52.

Retire the word "retirement" and replace it with a personal "renaissance."

## 53.

You are either moving forward or sliding backward. Life doesn't afford you the option of standing still.

## 54.

If you could spend a week with anyone from history, who would you choose to visit? Wouldn't that be a rewarding experience? Well, you can. Report to the library for seven consecutive days and read everything by or about this person you admire. Such literary visits will enrich you in lasting ways.

## 55.

Teachers plan detailed curricula for their students. Develop your own curriculum for personal growth. Study closely. Life experienced in this way always teaches lessons.

## 56.

Cast off "retirement" and take on "re-creation."

## 57.

Study creative works and the lives of those who made them. Your own creative juices will start to flow. That's guaranteed—because creativity is in your DNA. You just need to reawaken it.

## 58.

Don't think the grass is always greener on the other side, or you have unwittingly impaled yourself on the fence.

## 59.

Because the English language has countless words with multiple meanings, and scores of homonyms, we're blessed with the richest language in the world for humor.

The late Steve Allen believed anyone could learn to be funny. In fact, one of his books was titled *How To Be Funny*. Other comedy writers have written books on the mechanics of comedy creation. Read them. Practice time-tested comic formulas. You'll add sparkle to your daily conversations, and the playfulness associated with humor will infuse other areas of your life as well.

Keep a small, pocket notebook and pen with you at all times. When ideas, playful turns of phrases, or interesting observations come to you (and they will), jot these down in your notebook. Don't think you'll remember your thoughts—you won't. Get them onto paper. You're collecting creative kindling that will later light the fire of your imagination in uniquely personal ways. Try it and see.

## 61.

"Someday, I'll find the time…" is a promise we continually make to ourselves. Fulfill that promise now. *Make* the time. If not now, when?

## 62.

The quickest way to "think outside the box" is to realize this truth: The only real box is the one you create by limiting your thoughts.

## 63.

View any contemplated, unfulfilled dream as a determined tap on your shoulder.

## 64.

Nuggets of insight and wisdom can be mined from any situation. Be willing to prospect for them.

## 65.

Dedication to your creative spirit places you on a path different than that trod by most others. Some may view you as eccentric—even a little crazy. Good! Welcome and embrace these opinions as the great compliments they are.

## 66.

Creative soil surrounds you. Plant yourself in it, take root, and keep growing. Watch for attitudinal aphids of self-doubt, fear, and insecurity. Treat these with a liberal dose of confidence.

## 67.

Fail to see yourself as a miracle of creation and you take yourself for granted. Step back today to marvel at the gift of your life and its possibilities.

## 68.

Stop worrying about what others think of you. Most people seldom think at all.

## 69.

Ten percent of people reading this book would define themselves as "atheists" or "agnostics." They should turn this page now. It will not interest them.

I'd like to remind the remaining ninety percent of you: If God is *The* Creator, and you are made in His image, then creativity is a major part of you, too. By nature, you are loaded with it.

Delve inward and collaborate with Him today.

## 70.

Chronically discontented people spend a lifetime embracing shadows. If you believe your real life hasn't got started yet, you're finished.

Inertia inters ya.

## 71.

Ultimately, the greatest risk is in not doing. A negative attitude is really an internal life coach that keeps you benched from playing life's most important game—realizing your potential capabilities.

A friend of mine has a favorite expression which has become one of my own: "Too many people go through life 'shoulding' all over themselves." Full of fantasies, daydreams and unrealized longings, they never choose to act on their dreams. Time passes, regrets accumulate, but no steps are taken to move on their soul's urgings.

Make a "to-do" list of the "shoulds" in your life. Begin to act on them.

## 72.

Toss out "retire" and bring in "reexamine."

## 73.

Be less transmitter and more receiver. Instead of the repetitive, internal broadcast of familiar thoughts, be receptive to new ideas and opinions. You'll increase your learning to a much higher frequency.

**74.**

Think of comedians Laurel and Hardy, Jack Benny, Lucille Ball, Dick Van Dyke, and W.C. Fields. What do these talented people have in common? Apart from an ability to make us laugh, they all endeared themselves to the public through self-deprecating humor. We laugh at their frailties, ineptitudes and shortcomings. These wonderfully gifted, gentle clowns used self-effacing humor to connect with their audience. They established a solid, comic camaraderie that encouraged others not to be so hard on themselves. Their rich, comic personae and timeless humor remind us that *everyone* is a mixed bag of strengths and weaknesses.

When you can step back and laugh at your own foibles and insecurities, you'll no longer be limited by them.

**75.**

Be sure the only want that exceeds your needs is an insatiable desire for personal growth.

# 76.

While Abraham Lincoln had less than one year of formal education, a passion for learning consumed him. He was a voracious reader. Lincoln disciplined himself to improve his intellect. He mastered the English language. Desire and determination propelled him forward to develop strong leadership skills and foresight.

Use Lincoln's story as a powerful example of what commitment to passion can accomplish.

## 77.

Get off what you believe is the road *to* happiness and onto a path *of* happiness.

## 78.

The pursuit of happiness is a marathon chase, with never an enduring acquisition to show for your efforts. Nurture a passion that brings personal fulfillment and you'll make the pursuit of happiness unnecessary. Happiness will accompany you.

## 79.

Either dwell in the here and now, or count yourself among the world's homeless.

## 80.

Any success is a failure if you cannot fully appreciate it. Practice gratitude daily.

## 81.

The whole only *looks* bigger than the sum of its parts. Dismantle your dreams. Divide them into many small pieces, dedicating yourself to each part with patience and perseverance. The whole of a goal will never again overwhelm you.

### 82.

*None of us is ever satisfied with what we are.*
                                        --Terence

Nor should we be. Satisfaction with what you own ensures contentment. Satisfaction with who you are brings stunting complacency.

### 83.

Strike "retire" and choose "revitalize."

### 84.

Normal people are found only in fiction. Celebrate your quirks and eccentricities.

### 85.

Keep busy in good work. Make this your favorite leisure activity, and the joy of life will overflow.

## 86.

Commit to the goal of being able to say "Aha!" at least once every day (and mean it).

## 87.

Your value as a human being grows in direct proportion to how much you value others.

## 88.

Keep company only with those of good quality and excellent reputation—beginning with yourself.

## 89.

Be at peace within yourself before seeking friendship elsewhere; otherwise, you risk inflicting yourself on people.

## 90.

Foster the habit of glancing into a mirror each morning. Should you see your reflection there, know you have something to contribute this day.

## 91.

A friend of mine, Mike, has a standard, one-word reply to anyone asking, "How are you?"

"Thankful," he says.

Each day swirls with blessings when you live in perpetual gratitude.

## 92.

Develop an acute power of observation. It enables you to go deeper into the ordinary, enlarging and enriching your days.

## 93.

Think small. Fireworks may dazzle, but a solitary candle flame holds greater power to sustain connection with us.

## 94.

Delve into the unfamiliar. Welcome the chance to look awkward. Always be willing to make the mistakes required to learn and to achieve your goals. You'll be reminded, continually, that the well of your inner resources is bottomless.

## 95.

For joy and efficiency
Be content with sufficiency.

## 96.

Make full investment in this present moment. It will compound your interest in life.

(You may have noticed that this is my fifth reference to living in the present moment. There will be more. Dwelling in the "now" takes much patience and practice. The multiple comments addressing this topic throughout the book are here to encourage you to keep at it.)

## 97.

Just as youth is wasted on the young, too often middle-age is wasted on the middle-aged, and old age is wasted on the elderly. Your attitude determines the value of every stage of life.

## 98.

Your attitude fashions the past into a stepping stone or a millstone. Use reflection on yesterday to teach—not torment—you.

## 99.

If you knew your future, what would become of your enthusiasm? What would be your motive for action?

Treasure uncertainty. It's a better stimulant than coffee—and won't stain your teeth.

## 100.

Don't wait at the window for destiny, or you've already welcomed its arrival.

## 101.

Expunge "retire" and insert "restructure."

## 102.

Accept that life can be harrowing at times. If it weren't, you could harvest nothing from it.

## 103.

Exemplify integrity when you shut your front door every evening by continuing to be the honest, amiable person your neighbors believe you to be.

## 104.

Your spare moments are not recyclable. Never throw them away.

## 105.

It's what you do when there's "nothing to do" that can make a transforming difference in your life. The best use of spare time is to spare none from good purpose.

## 106.

If a blade of grass can force its way through concrete, surely determination and perseverance can move you, successfully, through any circumstances.

## 107.

Your hardest struggle in life may come in keeping yourself out of the struggle.  Focus on the essentials.

## 108.

Never argue with stupid people.  Willful ignorance is like pollen—you can't brush against it without taking some away with you.

## 109.

We often delay fulfillment of our personal dreams until "someday" when there will be time for them. Meanwhile, other life obligations consume our energy and attention.

Understand that "someday" will become "yesterday" before you know what's happened to you.  Pursue your dreams today.  Don't allow "meanwhile" to put "someday" behind you.

## 110.

Resignation walks away from failure and its broken dreams; persistence stays around to make creative use of the pieces.  Don't ever quit.

## 111.

Eyes see only what mind observes. True vision comes with attention to detail. Look closely.

## 112.

Find time for your goals the same way you find seating in crowded restaurants—by making reservations.

## 113.

Every human being is a marionette, with invisible strings attached between the ears. Pay attention to how thoughts control your actions. Keep aware of how thoughts make you feel.

Know that it is always your reaction to any situation that creates your mental response to it—never the situation itself. No outside circumstance can worm its way inside your head to produce unhappy, unwanted, or uncomfortable feelings. Your own thinking does that.

Catch any thought that makes you feel bad. Get into the habit of doing this, and your awareness of such thinking will slow the speed of your mind. You'll move effortlessly from a negative mental churn to a positive mental flow.

## 114.

Seek opportunities. Grab hold of doorknobs and take pleasure in turning them—whether you hear a knock or not.

## 115.

Creativity is best exercised by leaping over obvious conclusions and stretching your mind to think of alternatives.

## 116.

In each moment, in all that you do, beautiful creativity sits and waits—hoping you'll ask her to dance. Don't disappoint her.

## 117.

Understand that creativity is not some luxurious flower detached from the dirt of daily life. It gets planted between meals, phone calls, and visits to the bathroom, dug into the soil amid conflicts and crises. Your creativity grows and blossoms best in the ground of today's schedule.

## 118.

Encourage others to recognize that they are miracles in spite of what they think of themselves.

## 119.

Erase the word "retired" and substitute the word "resourceful."

## 120.

Before you ask another for a helping hand, be sure to fully engage the two you own.

## 121.

Regarding the use of time, ride that second hand and don't get off until you fall off.

## 122.

Some people struggle for years to "find" themselves, as though expecting their real self to show up suddenly, like a misplaced pair of sunglasses. Contented people never find themselves—they make themselves.

Create yourself daily through dedication to personal growth.

## 123.

Never try to be an imitation of someone else. Strive to be a first-rate version of yourself.

## 124.

If you're expecting perfection, you're on the wrong planet. We're all imperfect creatures. Despite our limitations, we possess unlimited possibilities and the potential for personal excellence. Focus on nurturing the best within you and tackle perfection in the next world.

## 125.

The best way to climb the ladder of success is to build your own rungs as you ascend it.

## 126.

*We cannot all be masters.*
          --Shakespeare

You *can* be master,

and should be—

of yourself.

## 127.

Spiritually uniform yourself to know that, whatever your station in life, you always outrank your circumstances.

## 128.

A scrawny self-image always produces weak results. While confidence doesn't guarantee a successful outcome, it does provide strength that keeps you in shape to lift obstacles out of the way, thereby clearing the path to your goal.

Self-disparagement is a form of blasphemy. Failure to commit to the life force within you, to build upon a sturdy spiritual foundation, dishonors the One who gave you all the tools to do so.

Trust in yourself.

## 129.

Until you can confidently ask yourself to the dance of life, do not ask anyone else. You'll only step on toes.

## 130.

Forget about life expectancy. What do you expect from yourself? Never mind how to spend the rest of your life—*invest* in it.

# 131.

Here's a photo of my mother as a girl, shown with her grandmother in 1929. Grandma Horner was just 62 when this picture was taken, but she looks considerably older. I think people of that generation acted elderly, too. Today, the average 62-year-old possesses a more youthful, vibrant self-image. Hurrah for this realistic change in view!

The young girl in this picture is now 27 years older than her grandmother was when the photo was taken. At 89, Mom still enjoys an active life. When I phone her, it's usually to leave a message on her answering machine. She's either out playing bridge, picking up books from the library, or spending the day running errands. How amazed her sedentary grandmother would be to witness this lifestyle. Stay active.

## 132.

How fortunate you are, seasoned by decades of life experience, to be able to detach yourself emotionally and assess both accomplishments and disappointments. You're uniquely positioned now to enjoy a more productive, enriching present and future, equipped with wisdom unavailable to you in youth.

All of the bonehead decisions you've made in the past are choices you'd *never* make again. Do you dwell wistfully on lost youth and the years behind you? If so, be sure to regret your inability to make the same mistakes and to wallow in the painful consequences that were part of your youth as well. Would you really choose to do that?

## 133.

No path of life comes with walls lining either side of it. Those exist only inside our heads. If necessary, we need to wield a mental wrecking ball.

Make mid-life a rest area to reassess both where you've been and the direction in which you're traveling. If unhappy with your current path, seek an alternative road. Plot a new course for the balance of your journey.

## 134.

Today's popular culture celebrates youth. Too often those in mid-life or older are perceived as no longer useful or worthy of attention. How ironic! Much of what pop culture chooses to champion is shallow. Be grateful not to be swept along in its vacuous flow.

Enduring cultural values involve wisdom, integrity, and the fostering of your creative spirit. Rejoice that you are perfectly aligned, at this age, to indulge in all that is truly meaningful about being human.

## 135.

Boredom, dissatisfaction, sadness, regret, disappointment, restlessness—these are all emotional alarm bells alerting you to the fact that it's time to take stock of the past, let go of it, and use the present to fashion a positive, productive, and playful life for yourself.

## 136.

To be at peace with the external limits life imposes on you, discard all the mental limits you place upon yourself.

## 137.

Life works best for the creative contortionist. When unforeseen circumstances thwart your plans, reshape and reformulate to adapt and move forward. Flexibility in the face of altered conditions brings strength and resilience.

## 138.

The best relief for the pain of unfulfilled dreams is a regular dose of compassion toward others—applied liberally. This prescription expires only when you do.

## 139.

*Thought is the sculptor who can create the person you want to be.*

> --Henry David Thoreau.

But only if you use the chisel of action.

# 140.

It's never the large action that brings real worth to a life, but rather the small kindnesses, the loving choices made quietly—day to day—throughout a lifetime. Think small.

Use kindness and compassion to make yourself a daily antidote to the evening news.

# 141.

If you don't feel the fire anymore, it's time to gather new kindling.

## 142.

Were I ever asked to give a commencement address to college graduates, mine would be the shortest speech on record (much to the delight of the students). Looking out across the rows of capped and gowned graduates—young adults filled with the desire "to be somebody"—I'd simply say, "Follow these two steps and you'll know success:

1) Ditch the desire 'to be somebody'
2) Know the miracle that is you and *be yourself"*

(I love this comment from Lily Tomlin: "I always wanted to be somebody. I should have been more specific.")

## 143.

In the pursuit of excellence, be sure what you've chosen to chase holds substance and spiritual significance. Never run after a goal that neglects your soul. To admire and appreciate the best life has to offer, don't anesthetize yourself to life's aesthetics.

## 144.

Focus on process, and the product will take care of itself.

## 145.

See to it that, when the book of your life comes to its close, the title is not *Don't Let This Happen To You.*

## 146.

Grow—or you will wilt. Your head does not contain a silk brain cell arrangement.

## 147.

Suggested daily prayer: "Thank you for this beautiful day, and for *every* beautiful day, regardless of the weather."

## 148.

Remember—the most important journey you'll ever make in life is the one inside yourself.

## 149.

Passion is the fuel that propels and sustains you in the pursuit of your dreams. Let unwavering commitment to your innate potential bind you to personal growth, and your fulfillment is assured.

## 150.

If your heart is not in what you do, the rest of you probably shouldn't be there, either. Discover where your heart resides, and join it.

## 151.

Never allow your core values to be shaken by challenging life circumstances, personal fear, or others' criticism and ridicule. Be aware of your real self— that the well of your untapped potential is bottomless. Trust that you can adapt and grow. Heart and mind engaged in passionate pursuits, wed by faith, make you unstoppable.

## 152.

You cannot appreciably alter the length of your life, but you do decide its depth—which is far more important, anyway.

## 153.

Never think of your past as lost; in truth, the accumulation of years and life experience have given you a full-time hobby of collecting yourself.

## 154.

Eat well and exercise to prevent hardening of the arteries, but also protect yourself from hardening of the attitudes. Chronological age loses significance with the realization that you're as young or old as the attitudes you hold.

## 155.

Benjamin Franklin said the way to get people out of poverty is to "make them feel uncomfortable in it." This holds true for extricating yourself from mental ruts as well. Let discomfort nudge you to change unwanted circumstances and move forward.

## 156.

Don't look...*see*. Don't hear...*listen*. Don't touch...*feel*. Don't taste...*savor*. Don't smell...*inhale scents slowly, deeply*.

## 157.

Journey with a sense of wonder, and all of your senses will come along for the miracle ride.

## 158.

Artist Georgia O'Keefe painted her flowers large, to make them visual "speed bumps," forcing others to pause and be dazzled by them. Slow your speed to the natural rhythms of life, and such magnification of beauty will no longer be necessary.

## 159.

Life takes its toll to grow your soul. Be still and wait in times of suffering and sadness. What will be revealed to you is a deeper meaning to your life than mere physical existence.

## 160.

Some people see the glass as half empty; others, as half full. Sometimes it's best to see it as a dribble glass.

## 161.

a) **habitual routine**: A place for everything, everything in its place.

b) **creativity:** More than one place for everything, everything out of its usual place.

To "b" or not to "b." That is the question.

## 162.

*Well done is better than well said.*

--Benjamin Franklin

Use the following advice, given by creative writing teachers, as a prescription for living well: "Show, don't tell."

## 163.

Creativity makes fresh connections. Practice unique juxtapositions of thoughts and objects to keep your mind nimble. This will feed your imagination.

Each time an idea is born, so are you.

## 164.

Use your reawakened curiosity to put boredom to bed permanently.

## 165.

Find joy in the moment or you'll surely recognize it in retrospect—with regret.

## 166.

Don't be one of those people who surrender to the enemies of fear, self-doubt and insecurity before the inner battle has even begun. Advance, with confidence, on the field of your dreams, and all opposition will retreat.

## 167.

*No person has the right to rain on your dreams.*

--Marian Wright Edelman

Your dreams cannot be dampened by anyone if you shield them with the mental umbrella of determination.

## 168.

Nothing holds real value until you connect with it through awareness and a loving spirit.

## 169.

Never succumb to live after another's opinion; true love urges you to shed any shyness of soul. It celebrates your unique spirit.

## 170.

By now, your habits and routine ways of doing things are probably performed unconsciously. Choose not to drift through the rest of your life unconscious.

## 171.

Foster your zeal or you'll surely congeal.

## 172.

Dreams are merely fantasies until acted upon. Take steps toward your dreams to transform them into visions—and reality.

## 173.

Inner evolution requires your enthusiasm and faith. Become an avid fan of life. The myriad possibilities each moment affords will reveal themselves to you.

## 174.

If, through a string of failures, you can bring innovation to each subsequent attempt, your success is inevitable.

## 175.

Postpone doubts and fears until you've exhausted all the potential excellence within you. You'll be a healthy procrastinator for life.

## 176.

To ensure that opportunity knocks, create the doors yourself and do your own knocking.

## 177.

Remember: The pursuit of happiness will always leave you winded and unfulfilled.

## 178.

There are no satisfying answers to life's biggest questions. Faith will prevent the paradox of this planet from paralyzing you. Embrace the question mark of existence as an exclamation point, and move forward through life in loving defiance of its contradictions. You'll help tip the balance toward the good.

## 179.

Combine playfulness with a sense of awe, and your creative spirit will soar.

## 180.

*To live is so startling it leaves little time for anything else.*
                                                     --Emily Dickinson

Embrace life intensely.  Apathy prepares you for burial long before the embalmer does.

## 181.

*Twenty years from now you will be more disappointed by the things you didn't do than by the ones you did do. So throw off the bowlines. Sail away from the safe harbor.  Catch the trade winds in your sails.  Explore. Dream.  Discover.*

                                                     --Mark Twain

Too strong a desire for snugness and safety keeps you anchored to sameness, in stagnant waters.  Don't discover, too late, that you've docked in the Port of Regret.

# 182.

*Every time we love, every time we give, it's Christmas.*

--Dale Evans

And you don't need to wrestle with those knotted strands of lights.

It's impossible to "get ready" for living. For too many people, though, that *becomes* their way of life. But there is no "On the mark…get set…" to life. The word "Go!" was shouted the day you were born. Don't allow starting line to become finish line.

If preparation were *everything*, nothing would ever get done.

## 184.

Grandma Moses put down her knitting needles at age eighty-one, because of arthritis, and devoted her remaining days to creating art. "I picked up a paintbrush," she said, "—and lied about my age." This vigorous New England farmwife produced her delightful folk art for twenty years.

During an interview shortly before her death, the celebrated artist said, "I look back on my life the way I look at a good day's work: It is over, and I am satisfied with it."

Live so as to be able to say this about your journey here. The inner peace that comes from having employed time and energy to good purpose will frame your life as a work of art.

## 185.

Climb a mountain of questions. That's always better than resting in a hammock of answers.

## 186.

Everyone falters in performance. It's only when you quit that failure takes center stage—so stay in the spotlight.

## 187.

View "know thyself" as more than a Biblical precept. It's your lifetime job description.

## 188.

You can never fully realize your potential in this life, because the reservoir of your inner resources is literally inexhaustible. Untapped abilities and creative expression await your diligent discovery. Make a daily expedition of yourself.

## 189.

*Every man has his secret sorrows which the world knows not; and often times we call a man cold when he is only sad.*

--Henry Wadsworth Longfellow

If we possessed an ability to peer into the secret self of every human being, the word "intimidation" could be struck from the dictionary.

Practice empathy.

## 190.

Cut loose the tethers of habitual thought and let your mind leap toward genius.

## 191.

Recipe for a wholesome life: Never buy pre-packaged thoughts and behaviors. Make yours from scratch, using only the finest ingredients. This process takes a lot longer, but the product created will be uniquely yours.

## 192.

*You gain strength, courage, and confidence by every experience in which you really stop to look fear in the face. You must do the thing which you think you cannot do.*

--Eleanor Roosevelt

Don't just look fear in the face—stick your tongue out at it.

## 193.

Abandon all attempts to put your arms around success. It is impossible. Real success infuses those who steep themselves in the spiritual.

# 194.

Nineteenth Century clergyman Henry Ward Beecher described the first hour of each morning as being like a ship's rudder, because it can set the course for the rest of our day.

Spend this time in inspirational reading and quiet contemplation. You'll ensure a purposeful course for yourself daily.

# 195.

Mind your own business. Take inventory often. Network compassionately.

## 196.

Merriam-Webster defines a practitioner as "one who practices; especially one who practices a profession." Be an inspired life practitioner: Sustain and build your practice of character and courage.

## 197.

You're not on this planet to make something of yourself. You're here to make *yourself.* The only construction equipment required is a humble commitment to your soul.

## 198.

Overcome the obstacles to your goals…or *you* become the obstacle.

## 199.

Accept responsibility for all your life decisions. You'll position yourself to create a new and improved product. People who think themselves victims of circumstance waste their lives just writing disclaimers.

## 200.

To believe what you've heard makes you one of the herd. When truth you seek, you become unique. Test and judge all things for yourself.

## 201.

A daily pledge to your aspirations lifts you from the enormity of conformity.

## 202.

No university offers a major in Awareness, because the subject can't be compressed into four years of study. It requires a lifetime of paying attention. Ironically, each moment lived in awareness earns you another degree.

## 203.

Acquired knowledge is good; however, like paint, it's of no value kept inside the container. Apply it.

## 204.

Powerful living is not unlike powerful writing: It comes through good editing. Eliminate extraneous activities that lard your day with distractions. Retain only what is essential to moving your unique story forward.

## 205.

A "has-been" politician named Winston Churchill became a national hero at age sixty-six.

After years spent in the political wilderness, Ronald Reagan succeeded in bringing his conservative principles to the Presidency—at age seventy.

Carl Sandburg wrote beautiful love poems well into his eighties.

Remain as young as your passionate purposes.

## 206.

*The reward for work well done is the opportunity to do more.*

--Jonas Salk

See your accomplishment of any meaningful task as a foundation upon which to build future successes.

# 207.

One afternoon I made a list of common ways we sabo-
tage our creative potential. Here are a dozen surefire
obstacles to successful living:

1) undervaluing yourself

2) neglecting your creative potential

3) settling for habitual, routine living

4) shrinking from challenges

5) allowing fear and self-doubt to dictate your
actions

6) choosing the wrong goals

7) failure to take responsibility for *all* of your
life choices

8) allowing yourself to be intimidated by
others' accomplishments

9) the misuse of time

10) failure to utilize the power of humor

11) the disconnect between positive thinking
and positive action

12)  your unwillingness to focus

Here's the good news: Because we place these roadblocks in our own path, we can also choose to remove them.

No one else can do your road work for you. You are a one-person construction crew, with no time to lean on your shovel. Take a positive approach to each of these self-imposed roadblocks to personal fulfillment...

## 208.

Believe in yourself.

Each of us arrives here a miracle of creation, possessing more potential capability than can possibly be realized in a single lifespan. Everyone is gifted with desires and interests, and the potential to develop these into talents and abilities—throughout a lifetime.

The strongest foundation for ongoing personal development is an unshakable faith in yourself, grounded in humility and gratitude.

# 209.

Know that your creative spirit is boundless.

"I don't have a creative bone in my body" is one of the saddest statements any human being can make. It simply isn't true. Holding onto this mistaken belief keeps you blind to your potential. All young children are riddled with creativity, and you were no exception. Imagination, curiosity, and a sense of wonder were constant companions. You may have allowed these qualities to recede, but they have not left you. Rekindle them now and watch your creative spirit catch fire.

People who complain, "I don't have a creative bone in my body" are functional atheists, no matter how religious they claim to be.

# 210.

Break from habit and routine.

People nestle into comfortable, repetitive patterns of behavior to establish a sense of security and safety for themselves. The price they pay for doing so is high: Their creative spirit grows dormant.

Humorist James Thurber warned us, "There is no safety in numbers—or in anything else." Don't allow habit and routine to create the illusion of security for you. Choose opportunity over security and allow *life* to become your safety net.

Habit and routine, inevitably divorced from imagination, always snub your creative soul.

# 211.

Seek challenges.

Don't view challenges as obstacles to be avoided. They should be welcomed. Accept them with enthusiasm and you'll build internal fortitude. Challenges are opportunities for you to adapt and grow.

Mark Twain once said, "It's good to take your mind out once in awhile and dance on it. Otherwise, it gets all caked up."

## 212.

Never permit fear, self-doubt, or insecurity to immobilize you.

We look at some people and say, "Wow—they have it together! How do they stay so confident and self-assured?" In truth, those who appear to "have it together" know the same fears and insecurities the rest of us experience. They simply refuse to let negative thinking slam the door on their personal development.

Does fear keep you feeling "stuck" in life? Well, unless you're the victim of some deranged taxidermist, you needn't stay stuck. Here are twelve ways to conquer crippling fears, transform your desires into realities, and keep growing young:

**Know you are not alone.** Whatever your fears or anxieties, take comfort in knowing they are not unique to you. Others have written about their experiences and can help you overcome self-defeating, debilitating attitudes, to enjoy a fulfilling life. The wisdom these people offer is as close as your library card.

**Treat yourself with kindness.** Don't worry that people look at you and think you're strange. We're *all* strange, and the rest of us are too busy trying to mask our own strangeness to notice yours.

**Face your fears.** Fear avoidance is growth avoidance—and worse. It causes your world to shrink as you experience ever smaller comfort zones. One nasty characteristic of fear is its fertility. Left unchecked, it spawns even greater fears and worries.

While fear can spiral you downward, causing increased feelings of helplessness, this does not alter the truth that you remain in control of your life at all times. Fearful, anxious thinking does not spring from nowhere. You *choose* to allow such thoughts to dictate your actions—or, more likely, your inaction. Make healthy, affirmative choices instead. A commitment to positive actions—even tiny ones—breaks the cycle of fear and negativity. You begin transforming yourself into a creature of *good* habit.

**Be in positive control.** Being in positive control means choosing to live in the present, not creating negative, "what if" scenarios for your future. Being in positive control means choosing not to blame others for how you think and act. Positive control involves accepting full responsibility for the power to choose how you will live—right now.

**See fear as a symptom.** Fear is always a symptom—never the cause—of self-limiting behaviors. When you change your underlying attitudes from negative to positive, fear becomes manageable. You gain control of it, rather than allowing fear to control you. A positive, determined approach to change breeds more positive actions. Your confidence builds. The motivation to push beyond fear and anxiety grows as you exercise and strengthen your mental discipline and perseverance. Positive action—*any* positive action—empowers you.

**Improve your body chemistry.** Chemical reactions in the brain create your fearful, anxious feelings. But what causes these biochemical responses? Your thoughts produce them! The way you choose to respond to life's challenges determines your biochemistry. Change your thoughts, and you alter the chemical reactions that produce feelings of fear, panic, and anxiety.

**See yourself as a miracle of creation.** Thousands of years ago we human beings were told to "have faith as a grain of mustard seed," and nothing would be impossible to us. That same Authority taught a profoundly simple truth: The way we *think* determines the quality of life we fashion for ourselves: "As a man thinks, so is he." Believe in your ability to make healthy, positive choices. Worry, fear and anxiety cannot build upon a foundation of faith.

**Know that you are always right.** When you tell yourself, "I can't do that," "I will fail," or "I can't change the way I am," understand that these statements are all true. Also recognize that thoughts such as, "I can do this," "I can change who I am," and "I will move from failure to success" are true for you, too—the moment you choose to embrace them. Whatever you believe about yourself and your potential capabilities becomes your reality. Use this power in positive ways, and life becomes full of possibilities. Take the negative perspective and you thwart your personal development. Moment by moment, you either nurture or narrow your potential.

**Be patient with yourself.** Live in the moment with a positive attitude. Set incremental goals and rejoice when you achieve them. Commit to the process of positive change. Realize you are "re-programming" your mind. Your habitual, negative thought patterns took time to develop. Conditioning your mind to engage in habitual, healthy thinking will also take time.

**Don't take yourself too seriously.** Everyone is a bundle of strengths and weaknesses. Accept your own flawed self with a playful attitude, knowing that you were born for personal growth and inner fulfillment— but *never* for perfection. There's no eleventh commandment that says, "Get it right the first time or you're out of here." If such a commandment existed, finding parking spaces would never be a problem, and there'd be no lines at checkout counters. Not one person would populate this planet.

**Become "eyewitness" to your excuses.** Catch every negative message you tell yourself and analyze it, asking "Is this attitude working for me? Does it help or hinder my personal growth?" If a negative thought is holding you back, dismiss it from your mind. Replace it with a positive self-message, and then act on it. You'll move from fear to freedom.

**Welcome failure as your best teacher.** If you're not experiencing some failures on the road to success, you're just stalled in a ditch. It is failure that enables you to realize more of your potential. The lessons it teaches are your only route to personal growth. Failures and setbacks are not only learning tools. They're designed to test your commitment to personal development. Think of them as Nature's way of saying, "So—how much do you really want to change? How strong *is* your desire, anyway?"

Some people look at their failures and transform these events into a personal lifestyle. Others grow through setbacks and see themselves as that much closer to success. Accept setbacks, learn from them, and move on.

You will never "find" peace of mind, because you must create it. Fate isn't what happens *to* us. It's something inside ourselves. It's how we choose to use life events and circumstances to mold and shape us into who we want to be.

You can't pull yourself up while putting yourself down with fearful, negative thinking. Commit to a positive approach to living.

## 213.

Who are the happiest people you know? Are they the richest among us, those with the most expensive cars and houses, the people with the greatest power over others? I doubt it. Happiness is the delightful by-product that accompanies those who are quietly going about their days engaged in work they love, often in service to others.

A highly successful cardiologist once described his personal transformation from unwise goal seeker to sensible one. This man's lucrative career had enabled him to indulge in all the material goodies life has to offer. He drove the flashiest car, acquired every costly technological gadget that came along, and devoted himself entirely to enjoying the high life.

One day, unexpectedly, this man suffered cardiac arrest. When doctors resuscitated him, he reported having had an NDE (near-death experience), in which he underwent a detailed life review.

Today, materialistic motives no longer consume this cardiologist. The car he drives now—which will turn no heads—has a bumper sticker affixed to it. The message reads: *He who dies with the most toys is in for a big surprise.*

Choose your goals wisely.

## 214.

Take full responsibility for *all* of your life choices. The strongest superglue in the world doesn't come in a plastic tube or bottle. Its powerful ingredients consist of just four words strung together: *It's not my fault.* These words are guaranteed to epoxy us to unwanted life circumstances.

Personal accountability is the only effective solvent for detaching ourselves from the superglue of blame. Bitterness, resentment and envy also dissolve once we take complete responsibility for our life choices.

The fastest way to advance toward the achievement of any dream is to hold yourself accountable for the "who," "what," "where," "why" and "how" of your life. It will empower you to keep growing.

## 215.

Stop being intimidated by those whose talents and abilities surpass yours. When looking at accomplished people in any field, know that you are probably seeing results—*not* innate talents. You are viewing people who have identified their passions and committed to them. No doubt they slogged through a lot of frustration, doing things badly so as to do them well.

To compare yourself to someone whose talent you admire is to equate an apple seed with the apple. Innate talent is too often confused with dogged persistence. Plant the seeds of your passions, devote yourself to their growth, and watch talents ripen.

## 216.

"Time should not be trivialized," said bandleader/musician Artie Shaw, "It should be used—because it's the only thing we have." With apologies to Mr. Shaw, we don't "have time" at all. Our only real possession is the present moment. Use it well.

An old man in a wistful mood once said, "Oh, how I wish I could stand on a busy street corner, my hat in my hand, and let all the passersby drop their wasted minutes into it."

View time as treasure and squander none of it.

## 217.

Positive thinking without positive *action* is just wishful thinking. Today—and every day—get off your assets!

## 218.

Psychologists guide their patients to step outside negative, self-defeating attitudes and behaviors, to examine them objectively. By detaching from situations emotionally, patients are able to see problems more clearly and make healthy mental changes.

Use the power of humor as an internal therapist. Detach yourself during moments of personal stress and turmoil and view these from a humorous perspective. You'll position yourself to replace negative responses with positive ones.

## 219.

My father often counseled me, "Don't be like the proverbial knight who jumped on his horse and rode off in all directions. *Focus*."

Life wants to interrupt us sixty times every hour to ask, "Got a minute?" The most efficient people I know are those who keep long lists of things they know will never get done. They focus time and energy on what's most important.

Fight distractions. Keep your eye and attention on the essentials.

## 220.

Direct your mind to useful thoughts. Carefully choose words and actions of value. You'll infuse every moment with significance.

## 221.

Maturity requires that we put away childish things—but not *child-like* things. Never put behind you the youthful qualities of enthusiasm, optimism and an inquisitive mind.

## 222.

Bring love to all your actions today. It will train and tone you for any task.

## 223.

If introspection does not flood you with humility and appreciation, you're not doing it right. Be sure there's no dunce cap of egotism distracting you.

## 224.

See to it that Good Will is more than just a place to find bargains.

## 225.

Understand this: In the long run, it will be all of your short runs that counted.

## 226.

Character actor Burl Ives was fond of saying, "No one is here long enough to say he truly owns anything." That's certainly true of material goods, but you *can* claim ownership of your character. Use purposeful actions to move beyond skin and bones and influence the life of everyone you meet.

## 227.

Keep basic arithmetic a daily part of your life:

> Count your blessings.

> Subtract all regrets.

> Divide joys with others to multiply happiness.

## 228.

Do a good turn today that doesn't involve a steering wheel.

## 229.

Act as a Siamese twin to everyone you meet—invisibly joined at the soul.

## 230.

Either all of life holds meaning, or nothing is of any real importance. There's no middle ground. Wed your mind to the first view, accept the inexplicable, and the goodness of life will always surpass its sorrows.

## 231.

Cemeteries are filled with people who once said, "Someday, I'll…" Procrastination makes a pillow of time and provides a head start in eternal rest.

Refuse to snooze. Time is to *use*. It's wonderful to be full of plans, but anyone unwilling to act on a plan is just full of it.

## 232.

Alter the ways that you use time, and you'll "find" all the time you need to accomplish anything.

## 233.

Commit at least one act of unadulterated silliness daily. It's the next best thing to finding the Fountain of Youth.

## 234.

If at times you feel bored, consider this a good sign. Boredom is Nature's way of pushing you to move in new and meaningful directions.

## 235.

The best of life comes to us in whispers. Lean in close or you'll miss a lot.

## 236.

Taking life seriously requires your good-natured laughter in the face of life's fragility. Laughter connects you to others and strengthens your soul. Look for humor in this day.

## 237.

How does your life fit into the cosmic scheme of things? It will fit any way you choose. Choose meaningfully.

## 238.

The shortest distance between two points is usually the least interesting way to travel. Be adventurous. You won't learn anything new if you don't *do* anything new.

## 239.

Make restlessness and discontent your wings, and action your take-off.

## 240.

Every thoughtful person grows confused and disoriented at times. Just be grateful you're not bumping into things.

## 241.

*Too many people die with their music still in them.*
--OliverWendell Holmes

At this stage you know the score, so share your melodies.

## 242.

Don't *try* to do your best today. *Do* it.

## 243.

Forsake "retire" and choose to "recast."

## 244.

A symphony is defined as "a harmonious combination of elements." This also describes a sound life. Take note of your movements and create a pleasant composition.

## 245.

Learn one new word each day. Write it in a notebook and revisit that notebook monthly. Words expand your palette for colorful thinking and creative expression.

## 246.

Sit at a window for ten minutes every morning. If boredom sets in before the ten minutes are up, you need to take a closer look.

## 247.

An algebraic formula for living well: If you can't be happy until you have "x," then let "x" equal the present moment. Otherwise, you'll never solve the problem.

Never postpone a creative task until you're "in the mood" for it. Creative work is always the result of commitment, regardless of mood. The happy truth is that dedication to a project often puts you "in the mood" once you're under way. Getting down to creative work brings you up to excellence.

You will never, in any lasting sense, "find" your groove. Life simply doesn't work that way. Grooves must be made. Wait for inspiration before taking action on things you want to achieve and you'll accomplish little. Time will be squandered in frustration and drifting.

Become an unshakable believer in discipline and the commitment to doing what you don't feel like doing. So long as the goal excites you, persevere. The inevitable miracle of staying true to a passion, of slogging through a commitment when you don't feel like working at it, is that *inspiration comes through the doing*. This phenomenon is called "flow."

An added benefit is the powerful sense of control that accompanies discipline in the face of distractions or the seductive lure of procrastination. Keep the commitment and you'll know true ownership of your self.

A fundamental life truth is that you cannot "try" to do anything. You'll either commit to doing something, or you won't.  Ultimately, the only thing holding you back in this life is you.

Look at any great work of art, listen to any beautiful piece of music, read any good book, and know that behind ALL these creative products was a person who, on many days, didn't feel like working at the project-- but did so anyway.  Commitment to an established routine--above all else--brought inspiration and meaning to the work and saw it through to completion.

### 249.

Mentally muss the hair of every sophisticate who crosses your path.

### 250.

Emotion usually reaches the finish line well ahead of reason.  In all your mental races, be sure your feelings come in second.

## 251.

Potential pervades you. Poke it awake for the sake of yourself and posterity.

## 252.

Be someone upon whose shoulders the next generation will choose to stand.

## 253.

If you feel the urge to lash out at someone, grasp the lash by both ends and use it for a jump rope.

## 254.

Be kind—even in your criticism. Kindness is infectious, cures many ills, and provides a welcome counterpoint to the evening news. Kindness is not more important than wisdom. It *is* wisdom.

## 255.

One dictionary definition of life is, "the interval between birth and death." You can do better than this. Give your life a definition that includes enough positive words and action verbs to fill a dictionary.

## 256.

Be a collector of people and relationships. You'll always have room for them, and they never need dusting.

## 257.

Inspect your hours. Be mindful of moments. In every second that you are awake, choose to *be* awake.

## 258.

Make this a boring day. Bore into it with honed perceptions, sharpened by sensory scrutiny, and you'll find it full of possibilities.

## 259.

Should you find yourself between peaks of enthusiasm, stuck in a mental valley, buy a trampoline.

## 260.

Abandon "retire" and adopt "reorganize."

## 261.

Life mirrors your attitude about it. Reflect on this.

## 262.

*Inspiration usually comes during work, rather than before it.*

--Madeleine L'Engle

Postponing work until inspiration comes is like waiting outside your house for a 747 to arrive in the back yard. Get busy.

## 263.

Youth sees possibilities; age, limits. Nurture your passions and you'll bypass chronology.

## 264.

All of us have an invisible key in the middle of our back. Your level of enthusiasm determines how tightly this key is wound.

## 265.

Years pass quickly for everyone, but they only become a blur to those who failed to focus. Center your vision on the essentials.

## 266.

Poet William Cowper offers this advice: "Squander your life for some good purpose." *Squander*? What an odd word choice. How does dedication to a worthy goal waste a life or spend it extravagantly?

With apologies to Mr. Cowper, I prefer this rewrite: Feed your soul by plunging yourself into some good purpose.

## 267.

With your mind you must huddle, or through life you will muddle.

## 268.

Take your cue from time: It never stands still—and neither should you.

A good way to keep your couch looking new is to stay too busy to sit on it. *You'll* look better, too.

## 269.

**occupy**: to fill up time or space

**preoccupy**: to engage or engross the interest or attention of

Which word best defines your approach to today?

### 270.

Should you prefer noise and crowds, always succumb to your emotions. If you enjoy solitude, go only where reason takes you. It will be so quiet there, you'll hear crickets chirping.

### 271.

Never waste time trying to engage the intelligence of people who refuse even to go steady with it.

### 272.

Life is not what happens to you—it's what happens *in* you.

### 273.

The best way to restrain explosive anger is with slow, deep breaths. These serve to lengthen your fuse.

## 274.

"Will wonders never cease?" They won't if your mind is open to them. Epiphanies surround you, waiting to astound you. See this day through captivated eyes.

## 275.

Prescription for perennial peace of mind: Never permit convenience to conquer conviction.

## 276.

Here's an oxymoron whose daily application will prove consistently profitable for you:

Plan to do something spontaneous today.

## 277.

The first step in putting hands to good use is to stop wringing them.

## 278.

Waste no time in trying to be better than you are. Realize the full value of your present self.

## 279.

Use the word "failure" only when describing a dream not acted upon. What most people call "failures" are simply the learning tools necessary to propel us toward our dreams.

## 280.

*Man does not simply exist, but always decides what his existence will be, what he will become in the next moment.*

--Viktor Frankel

Never to be premeditated is a crime against yourself (and condemns you as a prisoner of circumstance).

## 281.

Don't allow deliberation to cause hibernation.

## 282.

Recognize that, in the vocabulary of Life, you're spelling the word "destiny" daily.

## 283.

Revel in the small pleasures that life continually offers you. Distill your days to make them intoxicating.

## 284.

Awake with gratitude and you'll sanctify each morning.

## 285.

*And when is there time to remember, to sift, to weigh, to estimate, to total?*

--Tillie Olsen

You'll find the time in every conscious moment.

## 286.

*Clocks slay time... time is dead as long as it is being clicked off by little wheels; only when the clock stops does time come to life.*

--William Faulkner

The clock stops and time comes to life when you are fully in the moment—absorbed by something you love.

## 287.

To realize the full worth of each day, first grasp the full worth of yourself.

## 288.

Abolish "retired" and be "receptive."

## 289.

God exudes limitless, creative energy and shares it generously. Why just tap into creative spirit and siphon modest amounts of it? Don't be stingy with your self. Open wide to this energy source, with thankfulness. You were designed as a conduit for creativity. Let it surge through you.

## 290.

Push the wrongheaded concept of "luck" out of your mind and you'll clear a mental path to productivity and abundance.

## 291.

"Leaps" of faith are no longer necessary once you've learned to be still.

"Sometimes I sits and thinks, and sometimes I just sits," quipped baseball player Satchel Paige. Have you ever tried just sitting? Meditation is a marvelous means of quieting the mind—if you can do it. But it isn't easy for most of us. When you try to empty your head of all thoughts, your head will probably have other ideas— and lots of them. An incessant, internal chatter will distract you. Buddhists call this "monkey mind:" You jump from one thought to the next, the way a monkey swings from tree branch to tree branch in the jungle.

Yet, haven't you known moments when, not thinking of anything, your mind suddenly grew expansive, quiet, at peace? Even if the experience lasted only a few seconds, didn't it feel profound?

"Be still and know that I am God" instructs the Biblical psalm. When you "just sits," and your mind grows still, you become fully absorbed in the moment. Your mind connects with the spiritual. It is awashed with awe.

Take time each day to "Shush!" your mind.

## 293.

A large poster of Laurel and Hardy hangs on the wall in my work area. Stan and Ollie were my earliest comic mentors. Seeing them each day keeps me in continual touch with my kid self.

Reconnect with your warmest childhood experiences. Create a collection of favorite books (read them again), movies, and other items that evoke cherished memories for you.

Creative living demands that you keep one foot in your childhood for a lifetime.

## 294.

Creative consciousness transforms you into a spiritual stenographer: You're employed to transcribe the imaginative.

## 295.

Failure is not your enemy. It isn't meant to knock you down or out. View failure as a friend, one who takes you gently by the shoulders and redirects you on your chosen path.

## 296.

An entrepreneur is anyone who possesses an enterprise and is accountable for its management and growth. Entrepreneurs assume all the risks entailed in creating a successful venture.

*You* are an entrepreneur. The quality product you bring to market each day is your self, and you are 100% responsible for it. As your own boss, strive to be innovative. Are you willing to take risks? When your venture becomes an *adventure*, the business you create is guaranteed to be both profitable and unique.

Commit to your self and make a good living.

(I've found a great perk associated with being an entrepreneur: I get to sleep with the boss's wife.)

## 297.

Wikipedia defines "work ethic" as "a set of values based on hard work and diligence…a belief in the moral benefit of work and its ability to enhance character… being reliable, having initiative…"

As an entrepreneur, how is your work ethic?

## 298.

No one ever says "relax," or "calm down," or "take a deep breath" to a playful person. Silliness beats stress any day. Try it.

## 299.

Study the lives of Benjamin Franklin and Thomas Jefferson. You'll feel as though you're reading the biographies of sixteen people instead of just two. The word "genius" has been applied to both men, because they were accomplished in so many different fields. I think the common denominator shared by such people is a child-like curiosity—about *everything*. This youthful quality remains a dominant personality trait throughout their lives.

Follow their lead and you'll keep growing young.

## 300.

"Grow up" is, quite possibly, the worst advice ever given to anyone. Never take it.

## 301.

To act outside the box, stay out of box seating—don't be a spectator to life's possibilities.

## 302.

The only real, impending danger associated with a meaningful life change is that you'll let fear keep you from making one. Push through fear and keep moving forward.

## 303.

We can't know for sure what happens to us when we're dead; but, if you want to know what it's like to be half-dead, just observe humorless people.

## 304.

*I have treated many hundreds of patients. Among those over thirty-five, there has not been one whose problem in the last resort was not that of finding a religious outlook on life.*

--Carl Jung

Free-thinker Mark Twain once said, "You are the only Bible some people will ever read." That presents you with an enormous responsibility. Adopt an attitude of service, and the smallest of your actions will be infused with significance.

"Service with a smile" is no clichéd slogan. Make it part of your daily devotional. This is, in fact, your deepest calling.

## 305.

Never "play it safe," or you've chosen not to play at all.

## 306.

Make yourself comfortable as a beginner in every new undertaking, and you'll supplant self-consciousness with a consciousness of your evolving self.

## 307.

Whenever obstacles loom in front of you, weave them as threads of opportunity. You'll be creating a rich life tapestry.

## 308.

When somebody asks, "Where did you grow up?," be able to say truthfully, "I never did."

## 309.

The inner world of imagination is no escape from reality. Here you will find the birthplace for the best that reality has to offer. Take daily retreats to refresh your soul and deepen your days.

## 310.

Delete "retire" and select "refocus."

## 311.

What stirs you deeply? Move toward it and be not afraid. Forget about the less-traveled road—you're here to create your own road.

## 312.

Regret your past? Worried about your future? Neglect the present moment and you are neither here nor there.

## 313.

Negativity deters discernment. Patiently bend your energies to your desires and you'll experience clarity of vision. Prohibit negative attitudes from trespassing on your passionate premises.

## 314.

*One never goes so far as when one doesn't know where one is going.*

--Goethe

Travel far from habitual living and you're sure to arrive at new (and more interesting) parts of your self.

## 315.

Pay close attention to that part of the mind which detaches itself from your thoughts to observe them. This is your spiritual guide, here to offer you insights. Listen to it.

### 316.

Don't waste time outdoing others when you can be out doing for others something worthwhile.

### 317.

The lure of money, power or prestige will not hook anyone who understands that, when it comes to human souls, God makes no class distinctions. Choose meaningful goals.

### 318.

*Even if you are on the right track, you'll get run over if you just sit there.*

--Will Rogers

Loiter on the path of creative action and you risk becoming spiritual road kill.

## 319.

A two-part, internal workout to stay mentally fit:

> 1) always have dream destinations

> 2) take all the small steps necessary to arrive there

## 320.

Never pretend that you have it all together. You're much too small to be God—and you'll fool no one.

## 321.

Tear glands are provided as pressure release valves, and the moisture they produce helps to grow your soul. Use them.

## 322.

Unless you're masquerading as an antique quilt, don't stay sewn into worn out patterns of thought and behavior. Resilience enables you to remove the stitches.

## 323.

Psychiatrist/author Scott Peck once described life as "a celestial boot camp." Struggles and sorrows endured are meant to strengthen and enlighten you. Life is not designed to make you comfortable, nor is it meant to push you, in desperation, toward the spiritual. This world drills you to understand that you *are* spiritual.

## 324.

Using your library card to borrow and read Agatha Christie books is fun, but the most absorbing mystery available to you on loan is life itself. Keep your nose deep into it.

## 325.

Scrub the word "retirement" and substitute the word "reformation."

## 326.

Once you commit to creative expression and attain success, laurels sat upon will quickly feel like thorns. Achievement born of imagination produces a craving to do more. You live with a restless desire to tackle new projects, to engage in further exploration and discovery. Use your imagination to express joy and wonder in ways that bear your unique signature.

## 327.

Your schedule today contains important imaginative business. Keep your appointment with it.

## 328.

When your days are filled with playful exploration, interest may wane in the routine details of life. But crabgrass in your lawn is a small price to pay for renewed creativity. Besides, from an aerial view, all lawns look the same.

## 329.

See playfulness as Retinol for a wrinkled soul.

## 330.

Mentor others.

## 331.

*Most of the trouble in the world is caused by people wanting to be important.*

--T.S. Eliot

Ego always sends you sideways. Obsession with public approval keeps you a stranger to your best self. Should your ego begin to strut, throw a mental banana peel in its path.

## 332.

Share your dreams only with those who are living theirs. Seek out mentors.

## 333.

Shake off all sedentary thoughts and behaviors. Beneath the dust and debris of mindless habit you'll rediscover your five-year-old self.

## 334.

View chronic feelings of emptiness and frustration as mental shovels whacking you in the head. They alert you to the fact that you've buried your self alive. Grab hold of the handle and start digging.

# 385.

Any age is the perfect age to go to your room and play.
Do it today.

## 336.

Teenager Lucille Ball, enrolled in a New York drama school, was told repeatedly by instructors that she had no talent and should go home.

Aspiring actor Clint Eastwood was dismissed by a movie studio executive in the 1950's who said he spoke too slowly and that his Adam's apple stuck out too far.

When young Fred Astaire first came to Hollywood for a screen test, the critique was not promising: "Slightly balding, can't act, can dance a little." Fortunately, Astaire's passion and determination danced past all criticism to bring him a long and fruitful career.

Commit to your creative spirit—and sidestep the critics.

## 337.

Collect thoughts and ideas as ingredients for a creative stew. You can stir occasionally, but leave them to simmer. Your marinating mind invites a mysterious merging with the Master Chef.

### 338.

Creative thinking and instant gratification are incompatible. Imagination needs time to play with thoughts. To keep growing young, take in ideas and allow your mind to turn them over, move them around—mix and match them. Incubation often leads to insight.

Thomas Edison learned this truth and practiced it regularly. He studied a problem, experimenting with it in various ways. Then, with his head full of questions, he retired to bed, leaving all this information for his subconscious mind to sort out. The following morning, Edison often found himself awakening to a useful answer or to an innovative approach to his problem.

### 339.

Use sensory details to fill the creative well. Your well-being depends on it. Sensuality experienced in this way stirs you to recognize its spiritual core.

### 340.

Observe your thinking, and you'll come to understand that on every train of thought you are always the conductor—*never* the caboose.

"Follow your bliss," said mythologist/author Joseph Campbell. I've read this quote countless times in books, magazines—even on tee shirts and coffee mugs. While excellent advice, it's just half of what Campbell actually said. We're given a suggested action, but his promised result is omitted. Here is the complete quote:

*Follow your bliss, and doors will open where there were no doors before.*

I love the mystical quality of Campbell's promise. Be led by your personal passion. Have faith in the direction of your bliss. *Trust*, and you'll find benevolent, invisible guidance on your chosen path.

Let go of fear and surrender to the mystery. This allows the full emergence of your creative spirit.

## 342.

Merriam-Webster defines "celebrate" as a way "**a:** to honor...by refraining from ordinary business; **b:** to mark by festivities or other deviation from routine."

Sounds like a sensible way to experience the rest of your life, doesn't it?

## 343.

Analyze less; observe more.

## 344.

Dismiss your own thoughts whenever someone else is speaking to you. This will transform you into someone exceedingly rare—a true listener.

## 345.

Live in the present today. It's the best present you'll ever present to yourself.

## 346.

Busyness of thought transforms us into mental workaholics. If your mind is racing in six directions simultaneously, fueled by tension and stress, it is far too crowded to welcome any insight or genuine appreciation of life. A mind preoccupied with repetitive, recycled, rehashed thoughts closes itself to the precious qualities inherent in each day.

Theologian and Christian intellectual Reinhold Niebuhr wrote, "God grant me the serenity to accept the things I cannot change…"    Stress and tension are always red flags warning that you're on the wrong mental path. Serenity changes that path. It stops you from orchestrating, manipulating, and endlessly processing your thoughts. It allows their unfettered, creative flow. A surprising result will be your realization that much can, and does, change—for the better—once you cease being a mental workaholic.

Choose serenity.

## 347.

Grudges are self-constructed mental dams—guaranteed to impede happiness and creativity. Cling to hurts and resentments and you'll contaminate the present moment by poisoning the flow of its positive possibilities. Forgiveness relinquishes the pain and negativity associated with past wrongs. Use forgiveness to detoxify your mind.

## 348.

The present moment always welcomes you to immerse yourself in a clear, clean, invigorating stream. Don't bring along bad memories or negative thinking to needlessly muddy the water.

## 349.

Merriam-Webster defines "bondage" as "servitude or subjugation to a controlling person or force." The word "freedom" is defined as "liberation from slavery or restraint."

Creative thinking unfetters you to act in positive ways. Never permit negative, analytical thought to shackle you from the freedom of this present moment.

## 350.

Be aware of any thoughts that cause stress, and leave all agitation to the wash cycle.

## 351.

Slow and steady avoids the race and enables you to enjoy life at a "finish line" pace.

## 352.

Advertising promises satisfaction from the outside in. People literally buy into this false notion and accumulate lots of "stuff." Wisdom knows that true satisfaction comes from the inside out.

Settle into life with a contented mind. You'll keep free from clutter and spend less time dusting.

## 353.

Your life is useful in more ways than you imagine. Imagine that.

## 354.

Discard "retirement" and substitute "revelation."

## 355.

Choose not to coast, and no time of life will be downhill for you.

## 356.

If the law required you to wear a "mental nutrition label," what would your list of contents look like? Here's a healthy label to adhere to your product:

***Cranium Contains:*** *humility, gratitude, reverence, compassion, wonder, curiosity, playfulness, creative potential, confidence, optimism, simplicity, patience, discipline, perseverance, joy*

Make a list of your personal mental ingredients. Compare it to the one above.

## 357.

Invest in playfulness as an internal GPS system. With its guidance, you'll never lose direction.

## 358.

With the inevitable loss of loved ones, learn to let go with your mind, for now. Know that you stay bound to them by your heart forever. Love is stronger than death.

(We're all marching in the same parade. Departed loved ones were those out in front, carrying the banner.)

## 359.

People who continually seek instant gratification seldom express appreciation for what they already possess. Shun self-indulgence and know the contentment that accompanies a grateful heart.

## 360.

We attach highest value and deepest meaning to those objects for which we expend the greatest effort. Work most diligently for your own growth.

## 361.

Some people scoff at TV sit-coms from the 1950's and early 1960's, insisting that programs like *Father Knows Best, Leave It To Beaver*, and *The Andy Griffith Show* present an idealized version of family life. They're right about that. But these gentle comedies have valuable lessons to teach us. They provide a moral yardstick by which to measure our own spiritual development.

We can either strive to emulate that moral ideal in our daily lives, or see the ideal as "unrealistic" and dismiss it. Sadly, today's pop culture has chosen the latter course. Most sit-coms now celebrate human weaknesses and moral failings, appealing to the lowest common denominator.

Take a stand against the coarsening of our culture. Rent and watch *The Andy Griffith Show*. Carry the best of Mayberry in your heart.

## 362.

*Incredible the Lodging*
*But limited the Guest.*
                    --Emily Dickinson

Don't live as if you owned the house, and strive to leave the place in better shape than how you found it.

## 363.

When I was young, the scriptural passage "to gain your life you must lose it" puzzled me. But time and life experience have shed light on its meaning. The more your attention is turned to others, the less self-absorbed you'll be—and the more personal fulfillment will flood into your life.

"A person who has genuinely identified himself with other people has done something of first-rate importance for himself without intending it," writes Rev. Harry Emerson Fosdick, in his book *On Being A Real Person.* Prior to focusing on others, he has lived "in a mind like a room surrounded by mirrors. Every way he turned he saw himself. Now, however, some of the mirrors change to windows. He can see through them to new interests."

Use your talents and abilities in ways that serve others. Live larger than yourself.

## 364.

Eradicate "retire" and substitute "recharge."

# 365.

Goethe

*What you can do, or dream you can do, begin it; boldness has genius, power and magic in it.*

Timidity is a foundation upon which you can build nothing worthwhile. It becomes a solid slab under which you've buried your dreams. The overcautious, hesitating, and squeamish among us never take risks—and they eventually die anyway.

Assess the possibility of failure in any new venture, then adjust your creativity and courage to meet it.

Keep pleasant dreams.*

*And act on them *now*.  ("Later" always comes sooner than you think.)